NARRATIVE

OF

A VERY REMARKABLE

CONVERSION FROM POPERY,

IN

THE YEAR 1701.

EXTRACTED

FROM AN HITHERTO UNPUBLISHED MANUSCRIPT

OF

THE CELEBRATED

BISHOP BURNET.

LONDON:

PRINTED FOR JAMES RIDGWAY, PICCADILLY.

1822.

In the interest of creating a more extensive selection of rare historical book reprints, we have chosen to reproduce this title even though it may possibly have occasional imperfections such as missing and blurred pages, missing text, poor pictures, markings, dark backgrounds and other reproduction issues beyond our control. Because this work is culturally important, we have made it available as a part of our commitment to protecting, preserving and promoting the world's literature. Thank you for your understanding.

NARRATIVE,

&c. &c.

THE following curious Fragment has recently been discovered among the unpublished manuscripts of Bishop Burnet. In this enlightened age it seems difficult to imagine, how the domestic grievances of a French tailor could be supposed to endanger the tranquillity of Europe, and be used as an argument against the repeal of oppressive laws, affecting many millions of Protestants in France:—

" IN the course of this winter (1701) an in-
" cident occurred, which greatly added to the
" violence of the Papists in France, and tended
" much to increase the persecution of the poor
" Protestants in that kingdom. Shortly after
" the peace of Ryswick, a French tailor of the

"name of Le Clerc, with his wife and children,
"came over to England from Passy, a village
"near Paris, and settled in the neighbourhood
"of London, where, after a residence of two or
"three years, they found themselves not only
"involved, in consequence of their dissipated
"and extravagant mode of living; but the gal-
"lantries of the wife had become so public, that
"a separation with her husband became neces-
"sary.

"It so happened, however, that the private
"means of M. Le Clerc being entirely wasted,
"and those of his wife strictly settled upon her-
"self and children (a precaution, it seems, that
"her father had prudently used, in order to
"protect her from the dissipated habits of
"the husband, who had stolen his only daugh-
"ter from him at a very early age), a friendly
"arrangement took place between the parties,
"and M. Le Clerc taking a separate lodging in
"King Street, Covent Garden, the wife settled
"herself in a small apartment in the Strand,
"where she was enabled to pursue her gallantries
"without molestation, whilst her husband was
"entertaining a mistress at his own lodgings in
"King Street.

"In this situation of things, the two daugh-
"ters, who had grown up to woman's estate, the
"youngest being about eighteen, and the eldest

"about twenty years of age, found themselves
"very unpleasantly circumstanced, and were, in
"truth, greatly in the way of both father and
"mother; for inasmuch as the lodgings of the
"latter afforded no better convenience to these
"young women than a bed put up in the sit-
"ting room, they were frequently obliged to
"keep company with their father's mistress in
"King Street, with whom, indeed, one or other
"was occasionally made to sleep, and they were
"on the other hand much annoyed, by the be-
"haviour of the gallants who frequented the
"lodging of their mother.

"It should here be remarked, that as these
"young women had never been taken since
"their first arrival in England to any place of
"public worship, nor had received the slightest
"religious instruction of any sort, it seemed
"plain enough, that the intention of the pa-
"rents was to bring them up agreeably to their
"own loose and irreligious course of life.

"In the mean time, M. Le Clerc's brother,
"who it seems was somewhere beyond the seas,
"and ignorant of all these particulars, sends
"him over a young daughter of his, a girl of
"thirteen, in order to be instructed, under his
"care, in the English language.

"This additional charge, determined M. Le
"Clerc to place his young niece, together with

"his two daughters, in some place of education;
"and a school where boarders were taken, then
"lately set up in Great Queen Street, Lincoln's
"Inn Fields, and kept by two persons of great
"respectability, the one a married woman, and
"the other a maiden sister, was fixed upon, most
"unfortunately, however, for these two ladies,
"who were perfectly unacquainted with the cha-
"racters of Le Clerc and his wife.

"It has already been stated, that although
"M. Le Clerc and all his family were Papists,
"yet none of them, since their quitting France,
"had ever frequented any Popish chapel, nor
"had held any intercourse whatsoever with any
"of the Popish clergy then in London; and
"as they equally abstained from attending any
"other description of public worship, the two
"daughters had grown up to womanhood, with
"little or no sense of religion of any kind; and
"having left France at an early age, it was but
"natural, if by chance any religious feelings
"came across their minds, that they should ex-
"perience a call towards the true profession of
"the Gospel, such as they saw it practised in
"England, and which formed so striking a con-
"trast with the loose principles and lives of their
"own parents. But be this as it may, Le Clerc
"and his wife, having placed their two daugh-
"ters and niece in Great Queen Street, after

"previously assenting to all the rules and regu-
"lations observed by the boarders in that esta-
"blishment, and in particular to their daugh-
"ters and niece following, with the rest of the
"young women, all the religious instructions
"and exercises of the house, exacted only a
"promise from the two school-mistresses, that
"they should not be suffered to abjure Popery,
"without adding, howsoever, the slightest stipu-
"lation, or providing the smallest means for their
"being instructed in the doctrines of the church
"of Rome.

"After a certain period had elapsed, it neces-
"sarily happened, that these three girls had but
"little knowledge of any other religious instruc-
"tion than what was conformable to the Pro-
"testant faith, and being moreover in the habit,
"on all great festivals, of attending divine service
"with their companions at the parish church of
"Saint Andrew Holborn, it so happened, that
"M. Le Clerc's young niece, who it seems was
"a girl of remarkably lively parts, was adjudged
"the first prize in the Church Catechism, out of
"four or five hundred young women in the
"parish (at that time under the religious in-
"struction of a very worthy minister, with whom
"I was well acquainted), a circumstance with
"which both M. and Mrs. Le Clerc appeared
"at the time highly flattered.

"In the mean while, the tailor and his wife,

" being freed at home from the presence of their
" grown-up daughters, were enabled during
" nearly three years to follow their inclinations
" undisturbed, and indeed, excepting that the
" mother removed for a short time at first to a
" lodging adjoining the school, they seemed al-
" most to have forgotten their children and ward
" during this long interval, M. Le Clerc in par-
" ticular passing most of his time in France.

" About the expiration, however, of the pe-
" riod in question, a Frenchman in London
" writes to the father, that his interests are
" likely to be greatly hurt by the general report
" spread abroad of his having brought up his
" daughters and niece as Protestants.

" Upon this M. Le Clerc, whose religion
" (like that of most other French Papists) con-
" sisted in little beyond a concern for his own
" interest at home, mixed up with a certain
" blind hatred against heretics, instilled into the
" mind of every infant in France by the nursery
" tales concerning the bloody Elizabeth and
" her tyrant father, together with a frightful
" catalogue of Catholic priests embowelled alive
" for being of the religion of the barons of
" Magna Charta, and a thousand such like
" old women's stories; M. Le Clerc, I say,
" upon receiving this intelligence from his
" friend in England, makes a show of great
" anger, and hastening back from France, tries

"to do away the impression he was fearful
"had been made against him, by giving im-
"mediate notice of his intention to remove his
"two daughters and niece from the school.

"Alarmed by this sudden resolution, the two
"elder girls, who by this time had attained the
"several ages of twenty and twenty-two years,
"and who, having been brought by the ex-
"ample of their companions and the instruc-
"tions of their teachers to a due sense of re-
"ligion and morality, had passed, whilst at
"school, the only happy years of their lives,
"found themselves quite unable to reconcile
"their minds to a renewal of those wretched
"scenes which awaited them at home, and
"earnestly therefore implored of their father,
"that he would permit them to remain some
"time longer in the asylum he himself had
"chosen for them, were it even but as teachers
"in the school, as this would enable them at
"least to earn their board, and relieve him from
"that heavy charge; for it would appear, that
"M. Le Clerc was driven to the necessity of
"pledging a pair of virginals belonging to his
"two girls, in order to discharge their last year's
"pension.

"As a farther inducement, the two young
"women confessed to their father, that what he

" had been informed of, as to their being de-
" sirous of renouncing the errors of Popery, was
" true, having been instructed, in company with
" the rest of their school companions, *with his
" knowledge*, in the doctrines of the reformed
" worship; but that they had never been al-
" lowed to gratify their inclination, by reason of
" the promise made to him on this head by their
" preceptresses, and which engagement had been
" strictly and most honourably kept by them.
" With respect, however, to their young cousin
" his niece, they represented to him, that having
" been placed at the school at so early an age
" as thirteen, she was in truth ignorant of any
" other religion besides the Protestant, and ever
" since she had won the prize in Saint Andrew's
" church, with which her uncle and aunt had
" appeared so highly delighted, she had always
" insisted upon being considered a Protestant,
" and was so surprised and angry, when told
" that she must go home and be a Papist again,
" that she had not ceased to importune her
" school mistresses on the subject, imploring on
" her knees, that she might be preserved against
" the misfortune of relapsing again into idolatry;
" and more especially, she said, as she knew it
" was her uncle's intention to send her imme-
" diately over the seas, back to her father, where

" she was sure of never more hearing the Gospel
" preached, nor being allowed to see any body
" but Papists.

" Unmoved however by this reasoning, M. Le
" Clerc had the two young women home: but,
" as their then age and experience no longer
" allowed of their being taken to his own lodging,
" and associating as heretofore with his mistress
" in King Street, they were consigned to their
" mother's sitting room in the Strand, an arrange-
" ment, it seems, highly inconvenient to Mrs. Le
" Clerc, and against which she expressed herself
" in terms of strong displeasure.

" In this abode, exposed to the persecution of
" M. Le Clerc, who came daily for this purpose
" from his own lodgings in King Street, the eldest
" girl urged in vain her age, and consequent right
" to liberty of conscience under the free govern-
" ment of England, where, unlike to France, *dif-*
" *ferent forms of religion made no distinction*
" *whatever in the social intercourse of families,*
" *any more than in the common participation of*
" *civil rights and privileges;* and that, after all,
" she had adopted the only faith in which she
" had ever received any religious instruction.

" Nothing however could avail, and finding at
" length her spirits quite unequal to this conti-
" nued contest with a parent, she one morning,
" at a very early hour, quitted the Strand, leaving

"behind her a few lines, stating, that, unable to
"bear any longer the wretchedness of her situ-
"ation, she had determined on putting an end
"to the dilemma in which she found herself; by
"making at once a recantation of the errors of
"Popery, in the hope, that her father would
"then be induced to permit her to return to
"Great Queen Street, as soon as he should know,
"that every endeavour to prevent the step in ques-
"tion had become useless; and she added, that
"after going through the necessary ceremony,
"she would repair to the school, and there wait
"his pleasure.

"M. Le Clerc goes to Great Queen Street, at
"the hour appointed; but after waiting some
"time, another letter arrives from his daughter,
"apologizing for failing in her promise of meeting
"him. In truth, it seems, that after going through
"the ceremony in question her courage totally
"failed her, and not being able to bring herself
"to meet her father, she took refuge in one of
"the city hospitals, where, being harboured
"by the head matron with all possible tender-
"ness and care, she was kept by her for nearly
"six weeks in her own chamber.

"In the mean while the tailor becoming
"quite outrageous, applies to the French King's
"ambassador, and lodging at the same time a most
"violent complaint at the office of his Majesty's

"Secretary of State, at Whitehall, he at length
"obtained an order for some runners, with a
"search warrant, under the false representation
"of his daughter being under age, and having
"been seduced from her parent's roof, by what
"he termed in law French, '*rapt de seduction.*'

"These runners, accompanied by M. Le Clerc,
"began *by searching all the brothels* within the
"liberties of London and Westminster, in some
"one of which, he would have it, that his daugh-
"ter was concealed.

"In the mean time, however, the matron of
"the hospital above mentioned, becoming alarm-
"ed and shocked at the violent and disgusting
"conduct of M. Le Clerc, who had made appli-
"cations to every magistrate in the metropolis,
"and sent note after note to every one of the
"King's ministers, consulted with some clergy-
"men of high respectability as to what was best to
"be done; when it was agreed, that the only pru-
"dent measure under the circumstances was, to
"seek out for some third party of known cha-
"racter, who might quiet the real or pretended
"fears of the father respecting the situation of
"his daughter.

"There happened to be at that moment in
"London, with his family, a M. Romillie, a
"French Huguenot gentleman, lately arrived from

"France, whose name was well known to these clergymen, and it was determined to submit the whole matter to his prudence and advice.

"One of these clergymen, a Dutch minister, who had come over to England shortly after the Revolution, and with whose family I was a good many years ago much acquainted when in Holland, was the person deputed to make the communication required.

"This minister accordingly waited one evening upon M. Romillie, with whom however he had no previous personal acquaintance; and after he had recounted all the circumstances of the case, and produced evidence of the young woman's being of full age, and that from the hour of her quitting her mother's lodgings she had not ceased for a moment being under the most respectable protection, M. Romillie gave it as his decided opinion, that all the parties concerned in concealing or harbouring the young woman, subsequently to her so quitting her mother's lodgings, although actuated by the purest and most honourable motives, had placed themselves most unnecessarily in a wrong position, inasmuch as she being represented by her father (however falsely) as having eloped *under age*, from *his* roof, merely on the *score* of religion, it was

"made to appear by him, that abjuring the
"errors of Popery became a ground for forget-
"ting the first of all religions, *viz.* that of
"a child's duty towards a parent, instead of
"evincing, if possible, increased duty and af-
"fection, which, as all men knew, were incul-
"cated in a peculiar manner by the doctrines
"of the reformed faith. It was necessary there-
"fore, he said, that, in the first instance, she
"should return to her parents, and when the
"true circumstances of her situation at home
"were made generally known, that she might
"then without difficulty avail herself of her age
"and the protection of the free laws of Eng-
"land, to solicit from her father a subsistence
"under some more suitable and decent roof.
"M. Romillie added, that being personally ac-
"quainted with the ambassador from the French
"court, a man of the highest worth and honour,
"he would, if requested so to do by the parties,
"obtain from him, that all further proceedings
"should forthwith cease, and take upon him-
"self the charge of restoring the young woman
"to her father.

"This proposition being thankfully acceded
"to, the young woman was immediately re-
"moved from the asylum where she had been
"nearly six weeks so hospitably and tenderly
"treated, and brought to the house of M. Ro-

"millie, who, informing without loss of time the
"French king's ambassador of all the circum-
"stances, notice was sent instantly to M. Le
"Clerc, that his daughter was found, and was
"desirous of soliciting his forgiveness for the fault
"she had committed in not fulfilling her pro-
"mise of meeting him in Great Queen Street,
"after leaving her mother's lodgings in the
"Strand.

"On the following day, the disconsolate tailor
"came to the house of M. Romillie; but, to the
"surprise of that gentleman, *declined seeing his
"daughter, whose retreat he had taken such pains
"to discover, and it was only after several similar
"visits, and after the young woman had been
"nearly a week under the roof of M. Romillie,
"that it appeared there was no suitable home for
"her to go to !*

"Still, however, M. Romillie continued in the
"opinion, that to satisfy the obligation of duty,
"which every child of whatever age owes *primâ
"facie* to a parent, it was necessary that she
"should return in the first instance to her father,
"*whatever the circumstances of her home might be.*
"But, he said, that if, after a reasonable lapse of
"time, her father, agreeably to an undertaking
"which it seems he had made, had not found for
"her a suitable asylum, the very intention of the
"law, common to France as well as to England,

" which emancipates a child at the age of
" twenty-one years, a law of *protection* as
" well as of privilege, would be defeated, if she
" did not then avail herself thereof, and remove
" to some more decent and becoming resi-
" dence.

" It appears, that although the young woman
" showed the most anxious desire of obtaining
" her father's forgiveness in respect to the only
" faulty step, which her own fears, or the ill-
" judged advice of others had made her take, in
" not keeping to her engagement of meeting
" him in the school, her repugnance, neverthe-
" less, to return home was so excessive, and was
" overcome with so much difficulty, as to in-
" duce M. Romillie to apprehend, that there
" were still more serious reasons than she chose
" to reveal, for her shrinking with so much
" abhorrence from the roof of her parents.

" M. Romillie still persisting however in the
" necessity of following the straight-forward
" course, the young woman was conveyed to
" her mother's lodging in the Strand, and left
" in the sitting room before described, thereby
" closing up all free passage to the apartment
" of Mrs. Le Clerc, who took little pains to
" disguise her ill humour at this annoyance.
" M. Le Clerc, during this period, remained
" with his own establishment in King Street.

"As ill luck would now have it, the poor
"girl, unable to endure this situation beyond
"one night, and either forgetting all the pro-
"mises she had made to M. Romillie, or again
"influenced by friends of more zeal than judg-
"ment, once more quitted her mother's lodging,
"without assigning the proper grounds; by
"which imprudent step, she destroyed at once
"all the good that might have been reaped
"from the mediation of M. Romillie, and re-
"placing herself once more most unnecessarily
"in the wrong, furnished her father with a
"pretext for reviving the same unfounded
"calumnies he had before spread abroad.

"At the expiration however of about three
"days, M. Le Clerc receives information, that
"his daughter had taken refuge in an asylum
"for widows and single women, situated in
"Southwark; and immediately hastening to the
"spot, demands his daughter, but is told, that
"although willing to see him, she had ex-
"pressed her determination not to quit the
"abode she had chosen.

"Not satisfied, as may be supposed, with this
"information, M. Le Clerc insisted upon his
"daughter being instantly delivered up to him;
"and after remaining more than half the day
"within the inclosure of the establishment, com-
"mitting various acts of violence, the peace of

"the whole neighbourhood became at length so
"disturbed, that the affrighted women found them-
"selves under the necessity of sending out by a
"back way for constables, who conveyed the en-
"raged tailor to the watchhouse, and it required
"even some of the king's yeomen of the guard from
"the Tower, on the opposite side of the water,
"to restrain his fury.

"On the following day, a second assault was
"made by M. Le Clerc on this heretofore peace-
"able dwelling, with such circumstances of ad-
"ditional violence, that it became once more
"necessary to call in the assistance of some of
"the king's pikemen, and he was conveyed for
"the second time to the watchhouse.

"A week or two after this last affray, having
"learned, as it would seem, by some scout kept
"by him for that purpose, that his daughter,
"accompanied by two of the widows belonging
"to the institution, was going to walk some dis-
"tance from home; M. Le Clerc, with the as-
"sistance of a journeyman printer and the
"driver of a hackney coach, assaults the three
"women just as they were crossing the Mall
"in St. James's Park, and endeavours to force
"his daughter into a coach, but was again
"secured by some soldiers, who, attracted by
"the shrieks of the three females, came to their

C

" assistance, and M. Le Clerc was consigned for
" the third time to the watchhouse.

" Abandoning, after this, all further endea-
" vours to get back his daughter by force,
" M. Le Clerc goes to the chambers of M'Pher-
" son, the famous Jacobite lawyer in the Tem-
" ple, and having related his tale, M'Pherson
" instantly perceived the handle he could make
" of the Frenchman, by drawing up an inflam-
" matory petition to the legislature, in which,
" under the pretext of a violation of the laws
" of nations, and the protection specially due
" to the subjects of the French king then
" in amity with Great Britain, he might take
" that opportunity of insulting the government
" and person of King William, and the religion
" by law established, as well as every in-
" stitution growing out of the glorious Revo-
" lution of 1688.

" A petition was accordingly framed by
" M'Pherson, representing the complainant as a
" venerable father of a family, the pattern of
" conjugal and parental virtues, who, having come
" over to visit England on the faith of treaties,
" had by the base arts of protestant fanaticks been
" robbed of the society of his children, who had
" been torn from the endearing domestic comforts
" of his fire-side, and parental religious instruc-

"tion, and whose seduction to Protestantism
"had blasted at once all their hopes of rising
"in life; followed by the grossest misrepresenta-
"tions against the practice and doctrines of the
"reformed churches in general, and containing in
"particular the most impudent attack on King
"William's government, and the established re-
"ligion. This petition, among various other to-
"pics, stated, that the three young women in
"question had been seduced to the Protestant faith
"by the grossest artifices; and that the gentle-
"women, who kept the school in Great Queen
"Street, were in the habit of taking their pupils
"to the meetings of itinerant field preachers, at
"which the wildest enthusiasm was exhibited; so
"that the congregation, after being worked up to
"the highest pitch of fanaticism, commonly be-
"came convulsed, and after displaying the most
"frightful contortions, jumped all together with
"that degree of violence, as at length to tumble
"on the ground one over the other in a state of
"complete exhaustion. That several of the young
"women had gained inflammations on the chest,
"and other disorders, by this extraordinary ex-
"ercise, and others had even lost their wits.
"That the terrors, moreover, under which they
"were constantly kept, of being predestinated
"from all eternity to be damned, unless they

" could be made to experience a new birth, as
" it was called, and the variety of prescriptions
" proposed by contending spiritual empirics for
" obtaining this necessary privilege, and be-
" tween which it was impossible to choose, had
" nearly driven the whole school distracted, until
" at length a certain old woman having picked
" up, whilst sweeping a shop, a miraculous seal,
" found herself suddenly pregnant by the Holy
" Ghost of the Shiloh, and sold to each of the
" three young women, for half a crown a piece,
" a sealed passport for Heaven, which, on the
" assurance of a clergyman of the Church of
" England, a member of the House of Commons,
" and a learned doctor of physic, convinced them
" of the truth of Protestantism!

" Of such stuff as this the petition of M. Le
" Clerc was made up, but much more would
" have been swallowed by the Tories and Jaco-
" bite conjuring country gentlemen, who never
" left a stone unturned that might tend to upset
" the government of King William, and the
" Church as by law established. How it could
" have happened, that the House of Lords per-
" mitted a petition so full of falsehoods and ab-
" surdity to lie on its table, is greatly to be won-
" dered at; but the principal strength of the
" Jacobite Popish party lay, as is well known,

" in that House, and all the leaders of that fac-
" tion were delighted in seizing this occasion to
" vent their spleen and animosity against King
" William and his government.

" The petition was accordingly brought for-
" ward in the upper house of Parliament, and
" the previous question being moved by the Lord
" Halifax, a violent debate ensued, in which the
" Tories, acting with little or no disguise, evi-
" dently used the silly petition of this profligate
" Frenchman as a mere stepping stone; and
" several old cavalier lords, who had been in
" their youth stout champions in the cause of
" the Star Chamber, and were impregnated with
" a species of fanatical reverence for arbitrary
" government, and the indefeasible right of
" kings, stept forward and advocated the cause
" of M. Le Clerc with as much heat as if the
" recal of King James had depended upon the
" success of his petition; whilst one Tory lord
" went the length of hinting, that even a breach
" between the courts of Versailles and White-
" hall might be the result of any inattention to
" the domestic misfortunes of the petitioner;
" whose children's scandalous and clandestine
" conversion to Protestantism, by miraculous
" seals, and itinerant jumping missionaries,
" might constitute, for aught he knew, a legiti-
" mate ground for hostilities between the two
" kingdoms.

"But the worst was, that the Papists through-
"out France, having some reason about this
"time to fear, that the French King was
"thinking of restoring to his Protestant sub-
"jects the privileges secured to them by
"the Edict of Nantes, privileges which he
"had been induced to revoke at the wicked
"suggestions of his ministers, who now forsooth
"wished to shelter themselves under the ex-
"ample, as they pretended, of our great King
"William, a prince known to the whole world
"as the avowed enemy of all religious persecu-
"tion, and yet impudently represented in
"France as having broken the articles of the
"Capitulation of Limerick, massacred a whole
"Catholic clan at Glenco, confiscated millions
"of Irish acres belonging to his Catholic
"subjects, and hung an Unitarian!—the
"French Papists, I say, taking up the
"cudgels for their countrymen in England, soon
"spread all over that kingdom, by means of
"their accustomed channels, the Jesuits and
"Friars, the terrible account of three young
"French Catholic women, seduced in England
"by the infernal arts and sorcery of certain fa-
"natics, possessed by the evil spirit, jumping
"and howling on the highways, and frighten-
"ing numbers into madhouses, by the terrors
"of predestined perdition, and the necessity of
"a new birth!

"Small tracts were circulated with the utmost industry, filled with these and many such like dismal histories, ornamented with cuts, representing the embowelling of seminary priests, under bloody Elizabeth, the dreadful persecution and massacres of the poor Catholic natives of Ireland and of Scotch Highlanders at Glenco, the miraculous seal found in sweeping a shop at Exeter, and the wonderful miracle of the second Shiloh, with true portraits of the midwife and doctor!

"These, and ten thousand other such imaginary tales, which the Papists of the vulgar sort in France suck in with their mother's milk, excited on this occasion such a burst of horror and indignation against *Heretics*, capable, as they were artfully made to believe, of such barbarity and absurdity united, that they got up petitions from every part of the kingdom, in order to induce the French King to abandon all further thoughts of restoring his Protestant subjects to the privileges of other citizens; and were proceeding to far greater extremities, when suddenly, an anonymous writer proposed the following plain query, which operated like a charm in allaying the ferment, by this time beginning to spread over Europe:—

"'*Query*. If an English tailor had emigrated to France, and had chosen to educate his daugh-

" ters in a convent in that country, rather than
" place them in a protestant boarding school in
" England; and if, on discovering that his daugh-
" ters had become papists, he had presented a
" libellous and insolent petition to the French
" government, filled with the grossest insults
" against the established religion and insti-
" tutions of France;—whether the English tailor
" would not have been first heartily laughed at
" for his folly in not educating his own children
" in his own country, and by teachers of his own
" religion; and then kicked out of France for
" his astonishing impudence?'

" This plain query being universally answered
" in the affirmative, good humour was instantly
" re-established betwixt the two kingdoms. Jus-
" tice was at length done to the meritorious and
" grossly calumniated teachers in Great Queen
" Street, and M. Le Clerc was content to leave
" his eldest daughter at the asylum for widows
" and single women in Southwark, and to remove
" the rest of his family, from their several lodg-
" ings in King Street Covent Garden and the
" Strand, back to Passy."

THE END.

CHARLES WOOD, Printer,
Poppin's Court, Fleet Street, London.

Printed by Libri Plureos GmbH in Hamburg, Germany